Face To Face

Poems by
Julia Vinograd

Art by Chris Trian

Zeitgeist Press

Cover photo: Dave De La Vega
Cover design: Bruce Isaacson

ISBN: 0-929730-74-7

Zeitgeist Press
1630 University Avenue #34
Berkeley, CA 94703 U.S.A.

CONTENTS

FULL PAGE DRAWINGS:

ADVENTURE IN A NIGHTCLUB

In a packed roaring nightclub where the bands never stopped
there was a small dark octopus
hiding in the ladies' toilet
and reaching up one curly puckered tentacle
to grope the girls' bright bare butts
when they sat down.
The girls jumped up and screamed
but by the time anyone came
(it was a very loud nightclub)
the octopus had sunk out of sight.
The girls didn't know what had happened
but couldn't stop babbling, they sounded crazy.
Most of them got 86d for being obviously stoned
and causing trouble.
It could have gone on forever.
But once, when a gaggle of girls
were doing coke in the bathroom there was a raid
and all the drugs got flushed down the toilet
and the octopus swallowed them.
Then he didn't know what happened.
His timing was ruined.
After the next girl he forgot to sink out of sight,
just stayed with half his tentacles
waving helplessly over the toilet
while the bouncer's jaw dropped.
The manager called animal control
but before they took the octopus away
to some environmentally correct place
with no more naked bottoms
the manager took the octopus's picture
and hung it over the toilet.
He liked to think of girls
who wouldn't give him a second look
trembling each time they sat down.

PLAYING THE LOTTERY

I bought a lottery ticket
and before it didn't win
I was 2 people, me
and my fabulously rich twin.
She hired a limousine
and street people piled in,
shoving, hooting and hanging out the window
to give the finger.
We went to a fancy restaurant
that didn't want to let us in
but my rich twin slapped their faces
with a wad of hundreds
and ordered pink champagne for everyone
and roast duck flambé, caviar and just like the ad
all that cheese
which drunks smeared into each other's beards
and their girlfriends licked it off, giggling.
My rich twin, she bought out an entire Rolling Stones concert
for welfare mother's sons. Either sell the tickets
for 6 months of a better life,
the heat finally on, medicine, paid bills,
new clothes, schoolbooks
or one night of glory.
Never forgotten.
My rich twin, she bought a pair of senators
kept them on a leash and put them thru their paces
like poodles. They made laws like doodoo
when she took them walking in the morning.
The laws changed things.
Soon one-room residential hotels grew up
in cheap creaking dignity all over the country.
Old people sat in the lounge like bent umbrellas
telling their lives like Buddhist monks tell beads.
Sometimes I listened.
I bought a lottery ticket. No, it didn't win
but oh, the memories.

STAR WARS

The new Star Wars movie just opened
and I squeaked onto section 8 housing
but I think the government would rather use my rent money
to buy light sabers for every soldier in Iraq.
There's no stars in the wars here, often no light.
Darth Vader sends out pink slips
when factories close.
Why can't we have a soundtrack?
Boys who see Star Wars come out wanting to save the world
but walk past appeals for AIDS
and a drunken veteran in a wheelchair
sparechanging. His pants legs hang empty.
I can't help him either but I can make him a star.
In a galaxy far, far too near
he was going to be married.
She had red hair, freckles, no particular gift for silence
and she couldn't keep her hands off him.
His phantom limbs itch with the weight of her body,
there's not enough drink in the world to make him forget.
Sure, he stole his kid brother's train set once
and left it in their backyard beech tree.
The kid worshiped him, really it was sorta boring.
There'd been a job waiting
but not for a man in a wheelchair.
Can we put his face on a coffee mug or a t-shirt?
Once upon a time in a galaxy far, far too near
look what happens.
Where are the stars of peace?

BLUES FOR AMERICA

Sing blues for America, for big trucks
chasing the white lines all night
in every state on the mirror,
hauling heavy wooden boxes
nailed shut over our eyes.
America must not see. America, don't look
Sing boogie-woogie bug-eyed monster
uneasy to assemble blues for America,
will schoolchildren memorize the bill of wrongs?
Play spoons for nameless junkies cooking spoons
over a candle and America's greasy spoons
where nametagged peroxide waitresses call everyone "ducky".
Will government ghosts come to collect our names
while chattering waitresses collect our plates?
Sing blues for America.
High-stepping highways, fender kissing,
jelly-belly traffic jam blues for America,
fast cars, slow roads, leaning on horns.
A saxophone plays without pity
as pot roast and potatoes drift out of reach,
sing America drifting out of reach.
Sing rusty fire-escapes stretched
with laundry lines like fiddle strings,
walked on by mangy alley cats
and spangled circus acrobats.
Listen to laundry late at night,
boxer shorts and bathrobes sing blues for America leaving us,
America, don't go.
Drive-in horror movie background music
wails blues for America
with couples pretending terror in each other's arms,
knocking over half-empty popcorn boxes
and getting their knees tangled in the gear shift.
The 20 foot screen's full of blood and slime
but time stops when they kiss.
It's a small town, there are shotgun weddings,

but he's not to take his shotgun to war,
oh no, America, oh no.
Sing honky-tonk tacky blues for America.
Souvenir postcards of the Grand Canyon
with a Holiday Inn address on the back.
Give me some more of that old-time piano
and answer me this:
if we drop bombs just as deep all over the world
is the Grand Canyon still a wonder?
Will tourists still come with cameras?
Will we hear the center of the earth sing to the sky
or will we only sing blues for America?
Sing blues for a man standing in lines all day
and not getting work, coming home angry
and throwing a plate at the wall
because the food was overcooked,
next week he'll hit her
because he doesn't have work
and she's not looking at him but she might.
And he holds her all night
to hide from her eyes.
America, he thinks it's all his fault.
Sing blues for America, the land he loves,
the land we love.
America, come back.

THE VICTORIANS

Victorians covered the legs of all furniture,
otherwise it was indecent.
They might walk into a room
and interrupt a pile of chairs
sweating and grunting at all angles
topsy-turvy with the musky smell of varnish.
And if there was a fate worse than death
there'd be a litter of illegitimate whimpering footstools,
probably purple with gold silk trim,
shamefully bright.
Then the victorians went to church
and the preacher was so outraged by sin
the victorians felt they'd spent their Sunday
rolling with the damned on their bed of fire.
The damned were naked, young and beautiful
but the victorians were wearing their Sunday best,
high lace collars, long dark clothes
and sleeves tight at the wrist like handcuffs,
just in case.
The devils had modeled for gargoyles on the church roof
so hell was homey and familiar,.
As children they'd had nicknames for the gargoyles.
The ceiling of hell was open to heavenly hosts peering in,
wings and music watching the damned writhe so sweetly
in the arms of victorians wearing their Sunday best.
To look at God they had to look past Lucifer
with his tail tickling between their legs
which was not their fault.
It was easier to close their eyes.
Afterwards a potluck brunch and gossip.
Forbidden apples made into apple pie.
And women felt even the blind eyes of potatoes
in the potato salad
staring thru their clothes. Women blushed.
Men put on their black leather riding gloves, smiled
and left no fingerprints.

JERUSALEM WASHES HER HAIR

I saw Jerusalem washing her hair
in all the tears wept for her.
She stood under a roaring Niagara of grief
rubbing long fingers thru her dark wet prayers,
leaning her head back.
All faiths steamed over her shining skin.
Tears pounded down her bare shoulders.
Jerusalem took off a dress of broken promises
to wash her hair. All those betrayals
unfolding from all that beauty
which is also a betrayal.
We look at Jerusalem, want her,
we bring her funeral roses
and the weeping never stops.
Wailing voices kiss her stone lips
and the stones in her Wailing Wall.
Mothers rock dead children in a blanket of blood,
singing lullabies and little baby names
they've used for comfort;
if those names were on the death certificates
would there be as many death certificates?
Probably.
Suicide teenagers trying to marry Jerusalem, exploding,
their body parts thrown like bridal bouquets.
I've seen their pictures, they're all smiling,
surely youth can do anything.
Old scholars who turn their lives into nets of talmudic tales,
they usually keep their tears in wine bottles
but Jerusalem washes her hair
and they can't bear being old.
In ancient churches stained glass saints
weep glass tears shattering under Jerusalem's bare feet.
A farmer whose olive trees walked past the border,
the olives are ripe and ready for his hands

but there are sentries, he doesn't understand;
he gulps back a tear.
Even the guns weep and skeletons under the earth
who should've forgotten her.
Jerusalem washes her hair and rubs it
in a tangle of crumpled flags,
whatever comes to hand.
Then Jerusalem spreads it out on her hills to dry,
more lovely than her wildflowers.
Darker than any chance of peace.

HIROSHIMA

When I was in grade school
one of the teachers tried to make
Hiroshima real to us.
She wanted us to draw chalk outlines
around each other and imagine
that was all there was left.
Didn't work.
The pretty girls said mama didn't want
their good dresses all dirty and full of pebbles.
Teacher finally got a tarp and stretched it out.
And gave a speech about death which came from a book.
Then she passed out chalk and we started.
"Teacher, Annie's pinching my neck,
she says I'm not allowed to move 'cause I'm dead,
she's always picking on me."
"Teacher, Mary's rubbing chalk in my hair."
"Well, you always have dandruff 'cause you never
wash, what's the difference, tattletale?"
"Teacher, Jimmy's drawing too high up
between my legs, get him off me!"
"Teacher, Steve stole my chalk and broke it,
he says I'm not good enough to be dead
and I am so."
No, it didn't work.
The teacher stopped the game because for us
it could only be a game, played badly.
Like life.
She shooed us back to class
and before she went back to math
with the same chalk on the blackboard
she gave us a tight-lipped look
slightly out of focus.
I wonder if she was imagining a class
where all that sat at her desks were chalk outlines.
How silent. How peaceful.

RAIN

She's about 19.
It's raining because she has a new pink umbrella.
Her black hair's cut short and shiny
as her black dress with little pink nipples inside.
She wears black mary-jane shoes with pink bobby socks
to go with her umbrella that makes the rain.
It's not showers for flowers
like sentimental songs
or chilly moss growing
on the sides of coughing, homeless sleeping bags.
The weather knocks softly on her door each morning
when she's still sleeping with her mirror
and asks politely what she's going to wear today.
Wind to blow up her skirt?
Summer heat to open the cotton flowers on her dress
and the flower of her face?
Fog to hide her gray-white office suit
till only her long black stockings walk down the street?
She twirls her pink umbrella a little to the side
and lets cold rain run down her face
brightening her lips instead of lipstick
Men who can't get inside stare at her from damp doorways
and dream hotly of getting inside.
She passes them by but she wears their eyes
like drowned pearls. No other jewelry.
It's going to keep raining
until she gets bored with her pink umbrella
and gets a little straw hat
with blue and green ribbons around the rim.
There are no seasons anymore, no global warming.
If nature behaves as badly as man,
smashing twelve countries
I won't believe in nature anymore.
There's just a 19 year old dark-haired girl
sleeping with her mirror and telling the weather
what she's going to wear today.

FOR DAVID LERNER, DEATH OF A POET

300 pounds, laughing like the Loch Ness Monster,
about 6 foot 5 with 4 more inches
of a New York jewish afro and wide matching beard,
glasses scotch-taped together,
usually wearing green sweatpants
that made you look even larger and more rumpled.
You filled an elevator at Tom's art show
while horrified Warhol elegants clung to the corners,
their mirror shades ready to break
at the sight of your orange bowling shirt.
You were singing under your breath
"dum de deedle de dum".
You were so big
you couldn't quite fit in this world;
you had to make it bigger.
You shoved elbows thru history
looking for a place to sit
and rest your bad back.
You walked on your poems like Jesus walked on water.
You were almost religiously convinced
you could inconspicuously boost cigarettes
at the supermarket check out line. Oh well.
You'd occasionally proclaim someone god,
give them a 10 foot tall face filling your eyes
until you went for hamburgers
and forgot all about them.
The rest of us didn't exist
no matter how we squawked and yelped
until it was our turn:
"why didn't you tell me you were god?"
Totally exasperated as if we'd cheated you.
There was a bigger litter of lost gods behind you
than lost lighters,
and you always lost lighters.
You took advantage of your friends

14

and boasted about them.
When you got somehow rich you'd buy a big house
and we'd all live together
and have happy fights
and write poems hotter than the sun.
You didn't tie your shoelaces
and you thought people should prove they were worthy
to read your books.
You weren't patient enough for ordinary ambition,
you just wanted the sky to open
because you were a genius,
and the really irritating thing is
you *were* a genius.
You became a force of nature
by breaking as many natural laws
as legal ones,
sometimes you were chased by supernatural policemen
and demons.
Once you walked barefoot over the Bay Bridge
with 2 bags of laundry.
You rang my doorbell and said politely
you knew I worked for the Devil
but that was just my job
and would I look after your stuff
till things calmed down?
I gulped and said sure.
You were good with nuthouse phones,
you used them to fill phoney prescriptions
from imaginary doctors.
You made friends with other patients
like lost playmates from a childhood
none of you ever had.
You'd pulled your back moving furniture

which was a righteous reason to be strung out
but also you found junk lovely
and full of god.
Your lover finally left,
afraid you'd pawn her teddybear collection.
You were her biggest teddybear,
she wanted your children so bad
ghost children are playing marbles with your ghost right now,
you're probably all cheating.
You had a long rumbling laugh
with ships sailing across it;
they didn't always get to the other side.
You named your cat after a gangster,
wanted your very own army tank
to deal with traffic jams
and you even got a scrawled death threat
scrawled under your door
several months after you'd died.
Talk about immortality.
And you'd stand swaying in that packed back room
while we squeezed forward,
we couldn't breathe from waiting
and you knew it.
So you'd light a cigarette, slowly,
before your first poem.

18

DEATH SINGING TO YOUNG MEN

Come lovers, leave your flesh-flower girls
weeping on mattress dents you made,
moaning through their sweaty curls.
I'll hold you closer as you fade,
black blood dancing on a blade
and you will stay where you are laid.

Come lovers to my singing worms.
Burn in my bed as a city burns
naked of clothes, naked of names.
In my arms there is no blame.
I'll hold you closer as you fade,
black blood dancing on a blade
and you will stay where you are laid.

Come lovers to my endless dance,
you won't leave me here alone?
Clutch your girl but feel my glance
then let me turn you into stone.
I'll hold you closer as you fade,
black blood dancing on a blade
and you will stay where you are laid.

BE ON THE OUTLOOK FOR SUSPICIOUS
CHARACTERS ON PUBLIC TRANSPORTATION
(what we were told after the London bombing)

There was a girl on the bus
with an exploding brain.
The CIA was after her and so were slimy things
from other dimensions and telepathic ferrets
that climbed inside her skin.
And when she caught someone looking at her
she'd denounce them as mental patients
and tell them scornfully
to get back to the nuthouse where they belonged.
She always paid the busdriver in exact change
and carried 4 overstuffed plastic bags
that blocked the aisle.
I think they were the same 4 bags
each time I saw her.
Suspicious characters?
There was a young unwashed wino half asleep,
he managed to slouch against any pretty girl's shoulder
when she was caught between schoolbooks and the window.
She didn't see him coming till he squeezed in against her
and he didn't sleep past his stop
'cause he wasn't going anywhere.
She'd cringe away from his beery breath
as from anthrax,
and pray he didn't drool on her flowered dress.
Suspicious characters?
Boys in the back of the bus talking flash trash,
checking out bad sneers in black mirror shades,
big bad like their older brothers,
scary bad that gets girls,
they'll hold up a liquor store if that will get girls
but I'm not sure how well they hold their liquor.
Suspicious characters?
An old man with a cane and arthritis twisted muscles

has to crawl onto a bus seat very slowly.
Everyone smiles at him. He hates them.
He wishes they were dead.
Nothing to do with terrorism,
he's wished everyone dead for the past 20 years
and it's no one else's business.
Suspicious characters?
Like reading a murder mystery,
anyone, everyone.
You. Me.

FABLE

There was a man couldn't find a place
where he belonged.
One day he stumbled on an old-fashioned village
built between the naked thighs of a sleeping giantess,
the village church spire tickling her crotch
till she moaned a little in her sleep.
The villagers didn't know she was there,
at the most they complained about the weather
which was usually moist.
The man liked to go out at night
and watch the moon rising from between her lower lips.
Eagles pulled at her pubic hair to line their nests.
An eagle dropped a single hair at the man's feet.
"A natural redhead," he smiled,
"I'm so glad she doesn't dye."
Each Sunday he went to church with the villagers
and listened to the preacher condemn the sins of the flesh.
Afterwards he took a walk with a picnic lunch
along the giantess' outspread thigh.
When he got tired he pillowed his head
against her soft skin
nibbled on hard-boiled eggs and peaches
and wondered what she dreamed.
He built a small cottage close as he could get
and when it was her time of the month
he planted buckets of red hot blood in his garden
and grew the best roses in town.
Years passed. He didn't notice the years.
He didn't notice his own smile.

THANKSGIVING TURKEY GOD

I saw the terrible thanksgiving turkey god
ruffling his feathers
sprawled on a cold silver throne
while hordes of apron-stained, scurrying butchers
pour buckets of blood to warm his throne
and avoid his eyes.
His table groans with glistening soldiers
roasted on spits, grenades in their mouths.
With sushi savage lovers curled around each other,
still taking raw bites out of breast and thighs
before they disappear down the turkey god's steaming beak.
I saw a boiling soup cauldron bobbing with children,
squealing like piglets, pushing each other under
as they try to climb out;
will they drown before they're eaten?
"Praise me," booms the turkey god, and a dish of winos
still stewing in Wild Turkey try to sing.
The waiters were just on tv news,
they ask the turkey god
is he ready for bombed civilian families flambé,
for booby-trapped broken promises
and all the re-runs of MASH
suffocating under piles of mashed potatoes
with gravy of mushrooms and cut-out tongues?
He has only to say the word.
Later, there are gravestones of pumpkin pie
and the turkey god eats visiting relatives
with whipped cream and brandy.
They don't see him coming.
All kneel to the turkey god,
stretch your neck beneath his claw in awe.
Give thanks.
Give thanks.

BILLY THE KID

Billy the Kid wasn't kidding around.
He shrugged himself thru history like a human cactus,
all that paper tore at his touch.
A book of thorns, grinning when he emptied his guns.
I had a history book in eighth grade
that was so boring it would've put sheep to sleep.
I'd come home and I'd do history homework
till I couldn't bear it anymore.
Then I'd put the book face down
so numbing facts couldn't get out
and I'd go play with Billy and watch him kill people.
Billy shot people when he was drunk
or when they looked at him funny
but most of the time there wasn't a reason till afterwards
and it wasn't a good idea to ask.
Billy spun both smoking guns before putting them back
in their holsters and laughed.
He had a missing front tooth and freckles.
Billy ran his fingers thru his hair when he was hungry.
But I had to be back in time for dinner and history.
Memorize dates of battles and write a boring book report
pretending something happened in a war,
I can't remember which war.
I got older. I joined anti-war protests, marches,
speeches against senseless killing.
One night I dreamed of Billy the Kid.
He wasn't any older.
"Armies?" he scoffed, "these men take orders,
do you think I'd let anyone give me orders?
They're as bad as that posse getting up after me.
These poor fools kill people they're sent to kill;
a real man kills people he chooses for his own reasons."
"But Billy," I stammered, "you never had any reasons."

He looked at me as if I were crazy.
"I killed them because I wanted to, that's my reason.
Soldiers just want to go home
but they're stuck killing thousands more than I ever did
till someone else decides they can stop.
That's history.
All the books about it are the same.
If I was alive I might even join your protest,"
he winked at me.
"Killing should never be wasted
on people who can't appreciate it.
Send all the soldiers home
to take orders at work and sell things
and be polite to customers.
There's not many like me.
The wind is my country.
I'm pure as a rattlesnake.
You can come play with me anytime."

VEGETABLES

We were told to eat vegetables we didn't want
because of starving children
and if we didn't eat our vegetables
the children would die and it would be our fault.
I've seen lovers on the street
leaning back in shadowed doorways,
their bodies one sweaty smile from curled toes to tangled hair.
His hand half in her blouse, she tugging his blue jeans closer.
Time shatters around them like a broken beer bottle,
green shiny splinters in the sun outside their doorway.
And they're told they have no right to be happy
because there are dying children all over the world.
Sorrow is a vegetable, we're supposed to eat our vegetables.
Shame is a vegetable. Guilt is a vegetable.
We're supposed to eat our vegetables.
Lovers don't listen except to their skins
breaking on hands like the sea.
Even with their clothes mostly on,
they've taken language off
and just as well.
But sometimes I wonder about our soldiers overseas;
are they finally looking to kill the boys
who made them eat their brussels sprouts?

JERUSALEM MOURNS FOR THE DEAD SEA

"It's not like people," she explains
shrugging shadows away from her long neck,
"my lovers live to die in my arms,
my half-parted lips the last thing they ever see.
But the Dead Sea was never alive,
no one killed it in fierce battle
over my bare footprints.
It doesn't reflect my violet skies,
the fading colors of a bruise.
Its ripples do not repeat my name.
The Dead Sea is its own grave
and it makes me sad.
There should be golden fish flickering
thru my silver fingers, there should be water lilies
blowing on the banks of the Dead Sea
so I could pluck one for my restless hair.
There should be children making sandcastles on its shores
with toy soldiers to defend them from the tides.
My children die too soon?
But they die for me.
They're better playmates when they're alive,
pulling at my knees, talking all at once
and tumbling all over each other.
Then they're tumbling all over each other with guns.
I can't stop them but at least they were alive once
and knew my name.
The Dead Sea doesn't know my name.
The Dead Sea doesn't know I'm beautiful."

THE MASK

I bought a wooden painted mask at the flea market.
One face, but 2 broken mouths smashed together
and 4 bulging eyes sick with seeing.
The mask waited for the world to go away.
Children chasing a puppy in circles nearby
while their mother bargained for a necklace
with a clasp coming loose,
and a pile of indian silk glittering in the sun
like a golden lake
were more strokes of the hurting knife
that carved the mask
long ago.
Heavy in my hands I could almost see that knife
cutting the sky till it rained blood.
The mask had seen miracles, miracles changed nothing,
afterwards people had to eat
and they wound up eating each other.
It was a mask to hang on the wall, not to wear,
it was trying to wear itself out
but it had been carved too strong.
When the mask saw stars dancing on a frosty night
it felt like an old man in an empty furnished room
angry at the party upstairs with music turned on loud
and laughter, the man in the furnished room
works himself up to call the cops and make it stop
but who can the mask call to stop the stars?
It all washed over me. I smiled.
Lately, time's been made of tearing tissue paper.
We don't know how to plan past the end of the world
which they're selling on tv.
That marvelously ugly wooden mask
wants the world to end
and knows it won't.
I'll hang the mask on my wall.
It comforts me.

HUNGRY STREET MUSICIAN

Saxplayer, he can't eat music.
He sees an open air fruit market with bunched dusty grapes
and his mouth waters
while the grocer glowers at saxplayer's fingers
waving like anemones, no way he's got a penny.
The grocer's got an army of angels and policemen
to protect his rough-skinned pomegranates.
Saxplayer, he goes to the other corner,
dark eyes rippling like a wishing well
no one wishes on. Young. Freebox clothes.
Glory in his unwashed hair.
His hungry horn blows a long low note
cracking eggshells like Caruso's high note
cracked crystal goblets
and every egg in the grocery drips useless yellow goo.
Saxplayer, his next tune stomps ripe tomatoes on special
and drop-kicks a pink grapefruit thru a neighbor's window.
The window's owner yells at the grocer
waving the grapefruit for proof.
Saxplayer, the fruit market's too small.
His hot music roasts every bird in the sky,
feathers blown off in smoking blues,
brown sizzling skin, flying headless,
none of them fall to him.
His horn grabs gospel and the sweet Lamb of God
walks down the street on 4 cooked legs
with mint jelly and parsley.
And when the lion lying down with the lamb
growls at the saxplayer his stomach growls louder,
yeah, he could eat a lion,
but the tune ends without him getting a bite.
At the newsstand morning papers turn to menus.
He'd eat his own adam's apple if he could.
Saxplayer, he plays a library
filled with sandwiches instead of books

but he doesn't have a library card.
Saxplayer, when he'd first learned music
with enough wine to get him and his horn drunk together
someone mentioned a song can end the world.
Just talk, of course.
Saxplayer, he wants that song.
His horn smells cooked fish swimming in the sea out of reach,
garnished with breadcrumbs and butter.
He sees everyone else eating all over the world
and they have to be stopped.
Saxplayer, he's so hungry.
And his music's so beautiful
it goes on without him.

IT STARTS SO INNOCENTLY

When I was a child I wanted to fly
fiercely. I couldn't wait.
In the tub I'd get a crick in my neck
checking my shoulderblades for wingfeathers
wasted (as far as I could see)
on birds and angels.
Mother said stop squirming.
Airplanes were all wrong, too high,
I wanted to see everyone pointing up at me
and yelling.
I wanted to struggle with the wind
tugging at my clothes like an impatient lover.
I wanted to glow with being.
God was up there somewhere but he'd have to wait
while I picked the last ripe cherries
from the top of a tree.
I wanted to fly, not the airplane
that brought me peanuts, emergency instructions
and a movie.
Only bomber pilots fly that fiercely now,
low and deadly, metal wings too smooth
to be wasted on the angel of death.
The pilots are still very young
howling back at a howling sandstorm,
testing their muscles in hell
and thinking about girls ripe as cherries.
Pilots see everyone pointing up at them
and screaming,
trying hopelessly to get away.
Is that what I saw in the tub
when I got bubblebath soap in my eyes?

THE MONSTER

When they're fighting the drooling, towering monster
the prince and princess never fight each other.
No time. If they changed the subject
they could get eaten at any moment.
The monster threw them into each other's arms;
the monster's really Yenta the matchmaker.
But when the monster's dead
there's too much empty time.
The princess was as beautiful as the monster was ugly,
they were a balance,
but now her mirror has indigestion.
He remembers stalking the monster
thru a damp endless forest
and he's sorry it ended.
She does the best she can with the food.,
After each meal he silently forgives her.
They don't quarrel because they'd have to make up.
He spends more and more time out with the boys
telling tales of hunts and quests
and teasing Ted, for example, about the time
he nearly got seduced by a lady snake
and if they hadn't come along at exactly the wrong moment
he'd probably be raising a litter of garden snakes
at this very moment and teaching them baseball
if he could only figure out which end caught the ball.
She forgets all about him when he's not there.
Sometimes when he is there.
Once she thought she'd heard a claw scrape against the door
and leapt from her chair, a hand at her breathless throat
and a blush flooding her face
but it was only a wall creaking.

36

RUINS
(for the Sun Hong Kong restaurant)

Tourists go halfway around the world
to look at ruins
and check the spelling of the names of kings.
Sun on broken stone.
A tilted pillar holding up the wind
almost good enough for gods
who were no better than they should be.
History tears apart around a blessing.

I go halfway down the block
to a huge chinese restaurant that just closed.
I stare thru blind windows trying to remember
the bright brave tacky decorations
that made us happy,
a flag of bad taste waved against the moon.
2 sets of menus, one luxurious, costly
for dinner parties and one not.
But the cheap menu had the best roast duck noodle soup
for after a poetry reading
when we needed sunlight on our insides
after so much holding up the wind.
We were better than we should be.
History tears apart around a blessing.

Tour guides talk of centuries,
telling tales of what glamourously didn't happen.
Probably.
They watch for tourists' faces to turn young
and shy. Larger tips.
All tourist know of time is postcards.

I know less of time now.
The chinese restaurant was the only place in town

open till 2 am.
We needed an only to wrap around us
starting arguments about what glamourously won't happen.
Probably.
I see you all, the living and the dead.
Getting God and noodles in your beard.
Spilling love in your laps.
A girl's laugh rising like steam from the hot teapot.
My head is full of postcards.

LONELY

Lonely, he walks on the beach
and each wave feels the ocean turn its back.
Lonely, he walks in the graveyard,
in their coffins the dead believe
no one else ever died
and the worms are too stupid to care.
Lonely, he walks thru a forest,
the wind whimpers,
the trees don't trust each other.
In Lonely's shadow unhatched robins
cry blue tears in their blue speckled eggs.
Lonely, he goes to a park
where children feed breadcrumbs to ducks.
Lonely he watches and then he feeds
grandfathers to a grandfather clock.
Grandmother's too stupid to care.
Lonely, he goes to a girl's room
where she's losing a fight
with a photo of her boyfriend
gone to war.
She hates his uniform but she hates his smile more,
he doesn't look like he's thinking
about her at all.
He's too stupid to care.
She starts to cry.

ROOMS BY THE HOUR

Poems crawl over the floor
like cockroaches in furnished rooms
rented by the hour.
Dusty venetian blinds leave jail stripes
on heaving bodies while a poem
slips under a creased pillowcase.
Thin green soap in the bathroom sink
washes away fingerprints of all John Smiths,
John Does, names written in water.
Maybe their wives have names
but their wives aren't here.
The radiator growls like a pit-bull
about to bite the mailman
but there's never any mail.
There's a vacancy sign on the mirror.
The people here aren't really here;
they've got alibis and seven types of ambiguity
and parking tickets on the other side of town.
Cockroach poems wave their feelers
up the inside of knees that aren't really here.
Usually, it's the other way around
and people define reality by themselves.
But in this room only the poems are real,
scuttling little feet marching everywhere.

MARRIAGE POEM FOR A THREESOME

Come, celebrate a marriage of shining inconvenience
and a creaking bed spilling over
like a horny horn of plenty, soft juicy peaches,
breasts, and legs flying up to the ceiling.
Rollercoaster fights, delights, 3 clutching lovers,
2 cats, a kitten, a big terrified wolfdog
trying to hide under a small kitchen chair,
2 homeschooled children bouncing and running in circles
and a gecko; there's always someone
doing something wrong, stop that right now!
Anger, tears, the world ends often enough
to get the bends when the world begins,
giggling in Eden, let there be light to see you,
let there be sweaty rolling dark and hold me so close
we squash our ghosts that never stop talking.
No room for more button-eyed stuffed animals,
video games and books, there are always more.
No room to breathe except during kisses..
This is a marriage with various illnesses and pains
treated like squalling babies,
and this is a marriage that wants another baby.
It's all too much, it can't get enough.
And poems spilling over, climbing out of tangled sheets
and onto paper, showing off their sweet stains.
Clothes are only for dress up to leave the house
and go shopping; the fridge is always as full
as when she was snowbound back home
and no one knew when the roads would open.
And no one knows when the skies will open
and rain frogs or cooing doves.
All that organization, poetry readings, on the web,
a spider web for socks, strayed lighters and midwest memories
so mean to her she can't stop talking back to her ghosts.
But underneath she's shy as a bride;
don't let her out the door
without telling her she's beautiful.

DEMON LOVER

You can't bring him home to mother
even if mother were alive
and she's not.
You met him in a parking lot
when you were breaking up with some boring guy.
He looked straight across the parking lot
and laughed at you.
You took him home to prove
no one laughs at you
and gets away with it
and he uncoiled all over your bed.
And went on laughing.
You meant to tell him how insulted you were
but his forked tongue went down your throat.
In all this world he only likes cigarettes
and you, cigarettes remind him of home
and you're so good at hurting people
you'll be his assistant;
haven't you always felt cheated in this world?
Haven't you always wanted to get even?
He sticks a straw down your belly-button
and blows bubbles into you
like a kid playing with his soda
before he drinks.
You don't say anything.
He doesn't look back.
You're already waiting
for the next full moon.

STREET TEENAGERS BLOCKING THE SIDEWALK

One of them draws a chalk dragon on the sidewalk
with his blue green purple fingers.
His leather jacket's creaky as rusted armor
and the colors wound his knees.
People walk to their jobs avoiding the dragon's teeth.
His girl has blonde dreadlocks and her pet white rat
climbs in and out of her yellow silk sleeve.
Every time its pink eyes peer out
she leans down and whispers "boo" and the rat
scuttles back in and winds up clinging for dear life
to the side of her soft neck.
Her smile floats like a wished-on dandelion seed,
the next wind can blow it away.
Two grinning crouched guys drum on a garbage can,
their dirty ankles are slim as statues,
while a third guy kisses a winebottle
and sometimes his mouth-harp.
He doesn't look at a bluejeaned redhead
who's dancing her heavy breasts at everyone else.
When they get enough spare change
they'll make a dollar sign out of pennies.
They sit on the sidewalk, a plastic bag of day-old donuts
pushed from hip to warm hip.
They're blocking the sidewalk,
they're making building blocks of light and air
and then breathing on them. All fall down.
A passing little boy reaches pudgy fingers
for the rat's curling tail
and his mother drags him fiercely down the street
scolding in a voice like breaking tea-cups.
The chalk dragon drinks spilt tea,
sad for little boy fingers
that got away.

JERUSALEM AND A NEWSPAPER

A man swore hoarsely at his newspaper,
cursing her name.
He crushed his paper in both fists
like strangling a neck,
threw the paper across the coffee table
and walked out.
Jerusalem wondered,
and reached for his crumpled newspaper.
But at her touch lines of print
swarmed over her hands like spiders
dangling between her fingers,
sticky with spit and shells of dead beetles
while the sounds of battle shells
come over the hill.
Lines of print scuttled up Jerusalem's bare arms.
ready to bite.
She tried to dust them off
but there were so many.
At last she grabbed a coffee cup
from someone else's table
and soaked the newspaper till all the print ran away
leaving only a limp brown mush
around limp dead bodies.
Jerusalem's hands were free again.
She ran her fingers thru her tangled prayers,
washed herself in dreams,
and kissed her own wrists in relief.
"What do you think of what you read?" asked the Lord.
"How could I read, it was all over me," protested Jerusalem,
checking to make sure no words were left
under her fingernails like dried blood.
"Who reads spiderwebs anyway,
except crazy fools like that rude man?"
"I do," answered the Lord.
"I wrote every one."

THE KILLER WAVE, for the tsunami

Can we drive an army of copcars
and arrest the ocean?
Can we make each wave wear an orange prison jump suit
and stand in the dock and listen to charges
while a court sketch artist draws the sea?
Shop burglaries are often caught on spy cameras,
we have tourist videos
proving that crashing wall of water
is without a reasonable doubt guilty
but we don't have a big enough jail.
Do we handcuff fishes that don't have any hands?
We have 12 countries of bereaved witnesses,
each wanting justice for their own deceased.
The cold-blooded, cold water murder
with malice aforethought of all those children
who couldn't run fast enough;
when their parents try to sleep
do they dream of getting their hands around a neck
and squeezing? Any neck?
If the prosecutor read a list of the victims' names
he couldn't finish till we'd all died of old age.
Will the defense attorney show picture postcards
of ocean resorts and fishing villages
and put the attack down to temporary insanity
due to resurfacing memories of child abuse
disguised as an earthquake?
Or will a long-drowned layer come back to partial life,
half wrapped in sea-weed, a briefcase full of shells
and claim it was simply a traffic accident
and the ocean had the right of way?
And then ruin his case by remarking
it's not as if people are very important.
We've spent a year with tabloids, attack articles
and interviews with experts about whether a man

killed his pregnant wife on christmas eve
to be with his lover. The unholy family
and no one lost interest.
Are we letting the sea sink out of sight
just because there's no one face to point at and blame
shouting he did it, make him pay,
don't let him get away with it?
The ocean also attacked on christmas
and a grief stricken mob can't even burn it in effigy.
Call flies to the witness stand to testify
how the dead tasted, open eyeballs,
open mouths, swollen, succulent tongues.
Make us too sick to forget, gory details,
protective half masks and still the doctors gag.
Mangled stinking corpses not even hidden, no shame.
Our killer madmen foam at the mouth,
the ocean foams on the sand.
Its shining shameless tides
laugh at us under the full moon.

DRUMMERS

Circle of drummers, big hands, spilled red wine.
Breaking and entering a dictionary,
knocking all words into a senseless heap,
raping the clocks.
The time it takes a bead of sweat to roll
from a drummer's glistening black collarbone
to his belly-button
is the only time left.
A girl with cheap bright bracelets
jingling up both arms
and colored beads in her hair
holds her tambourine hummingbird still above her head
and throws her body about beneath it.
Her breasts aren't speaking to each other
and her whirling, scarlet-skirted knees
are parting company.
A passing guy half leans off his bicycle
flourishing a kazoo from his jeans' back pocket,
a whoopee cushion of the gods
squawking among drums that won't let him go.
The drums won't let the crowd go either,
nooses of sound pulled tight around their necks
like a herd rustled from their owners' schedules.
No jobs here, no homes, no promises.
Drums eat their names and they don't care.
A young guy cracks a wolf grin
and abuses his bruised clarinet.
Copcars wail down the sky
after drummers driving with an open container
and the genie half out.
After baby joy dribbling down his dimple
without a license.
Demonic possession with intent to sell popcorn.
Loitering at the Pearly Gates
to bum smokes.

FOR THE DEATH OF A FRIEND'S SON

Ben jr., captain. Dead. Blown up in Iraq.
That's all I know.
Your father wants a poem.
I know him as Ben, not Ben senior.
Your death hurts more than the war,
how can he think about politics?
He's thinking about the last time he saw you
and what you both said and didn't say
and should've said and all gone now,
all gone.
Or when you decided you were too old
for a baby name he gave you
or an argument about a friend or a girl
or how homecooking was just for kids.
But you always knew your Dad would be there for you
no matter what you both said.
You died alone.
You died alone.
He blames himself. He loves you.
You'd be indignant, you were your own man
not just someone's son.
But I'm writing this poem for someone's son,
and yes, you loved him
no matter what you both said.

CITY, SHE DANCES THE BLUES

City, she dances the blues.
She's a tear made flesh, fingers trembling to fog,
fog trembling to fingers.
City, she nibbles her twisty streets like pretzels,
then sticks a thumb in her drink
and sucks it like a baby.
It's a hot night.
Old buildings sweat but her skin's as cool
as a liar's face.
City, she dances the blues, the daily news,
gravestones with our morning coffee
and tip the waitress.
The what-went-wrong song
just one more thing we don't hear
like drilling in the street.
Plaster-dusted construction workers keep unfolding ladders
till they can pin the stars in City's heavy hair.
They laugh and argue the baseball game
thudding a meaty fist against a palm.
They don't look at her.
Construction workers talk about the time
they made the nipples on the Statue of Liberty harden.
Later they'll talk about her,
how their hands in City's hair
pulled her gasping against their knees.
But not now.
City, she dances the blues
coming unglued in smoky nightclubs,
bulldozers on her breath. We don't look.
We can't stop looking.
A young guy's mouth harp grew
an extra set of teeth nibbling at his lower lip.
In this room only the false IDs are true.
City, she leans over a fat man playing a quavering saw

in a midnight BART station,
City shows him a chainsaw massacre
of rude people who shoved him in a grocery store line.
Afterwards, his music's much better.
City, she dances the blues.
She's got this bruised look
makes everyone call "come back"
long before she leaves.
But it's not City we're calling
and no one comes.

SAND CASTLE

A 5 year old boy on the beach builds a sandcastle
with a red tin shovel and a red bucket.
His sun burnt nose is starting to peel.
The boy adds moats and walls
to protect his castle from the sea.
He bites his lip with concentration,
firming up the walls with shiny bits of shells
and filling his bucket with packed wet sand
for the rectangular towers.
They make a satisfactory thunk
when he pushes them into place,
drawing windows in the towers for archers
to shoot arrows into the sea.
He can almost hear the military trumpets.
His older brother's away at war;
the boy saw a picture of war once in a history book.
He liked the trumpets and the prancing horses.
He's nearly done. He uses a torn cigarette wrapping,
wrinkled tinsel, for a flag.
It catches the light.
Finally the boy writes his name in the sand
in front of his castle.
Surely the ocean knows his name.
To be absolutely positive he underlines his name
with one pudgy wavering finger.
But even the boy knows
only the sea lives in his castle.
Only the wind lives in the war.

WANTED POSTER

I saw God's face on a wanted poster.
"Dead or Alive. Armed and Dangerous."
The picture wasn't very good
but I've seen armies thrashing
thru the jungle of that eyebrow.
That mouth spat oceans on Sunday
like rank chewing tobacco.
Those hands threw wrinkles all over pretty women
and watched their breasts sag.
Indecent exposure of God's eyes.
Something must be done.
The poster offers big reward. Many crimes.
Creating and killing people without a license.
Without instructions or excuses.
Many jailbreaks from different holy books,
their covers locked like iron bars around God
but torn like paper behind his back.
Blessing the forest and blessing the forest fire.
The wanted poster didn't know what it wanted
but it was tired of God
looking over its shoulder
and laughing.

56

DAY OF A POEM

I saw a poem screaming on the street,
he'd just been in a fight with History.
History insulted the poem's mother
but History lies,
everyone knows History lies.
The poem has a bloody nose
and never had a mother.
A small noisy dog barks at the poem,
pulling at its leash, wanting to bite.
The poem barks back.
A teenage girl calls her dog and sniffs.
The poem doesn't give a damn about her ankles,
it's not that kind of day.
I saw a poem stirring a map with a spoon.
I saw a poem just back from the war
trying to lead a protest march of pigeons
thru the golden arches of McDonalds.
"afterwards, we'll all go splutz famous statues,"
he promised. "I know where they hide."
The pigeons pretended he wasn't there,
that happens to the poem a lot.
I saw a poem heading for a weatherbeaten shop,
the sign said "repairs while you wait".
The poem carried the world under one arm
and wiped off blood with his sleeve.
"See that sign?" the poem pointed
"everything will be all right."
The world didn't listen and the poem got bored.
There were some kids down the street
chanting jump rope songs and the poem joined them
scattering golden petals of the sun
under their tennis shoes.

IMPRESSIONS OF A YOUNG STREET GUY

Orchids with stuck out tongues twine
thru his torn t-shirt, licking his freckles,
almost licking them off.
He's about 20. Depending.
Time's a rubber band; it stretches and knots
in his long fingers, sometimes it breaks.
He wears the rain forest out in the rain.
Chattering, red-bottomed monkeys dangle
from the low-slung chains around his slim hips.
He scratches their tufted ears
and guards his cigarette from their grabby paws
when he has a cigarette. Not often.
He moves as if pink flamingoes bruise their beaks
inside his rib cage. There's parrots in his pockets.
Not much else. Bluegreen crested and cursing
in languages the young guy never heard.
He doesn't listen. Or to people much.
He got a newspaper once to spread
on a wet bench in the rain
while he peeled an orange with his pocket knife.
He didn't read the newspaper.
Those wars aren't his wars
and his world goes from his skin outward.
He's a graceful shrug made almost human.
There are lush flowers so deep in the rain forest
no one ever sees them.
Look at him, before he fades.

59

MONEY

Money, she's not as young as she used to be
but she's much better looking
at least from a distance.
Money, she wears a double looped necklace of false pearls
over the bare untruth of flesh
and we measure ourselves by her interest.
Money, she takes a clock for walks on a leash,
there's a bell on its collar
and a bow on its tail and it bites.
When she's done with her lovers she drops them
in mailboxes without an address.
Not her problem.
Money, of course she believes in charity.
She wears a black evening gown
and elbow length black velvet gloves
and pitches pennies
towards a street crazy's screaming throat
like feeding ducks in the park.
He's indecently exposing his tonsils
and Money, she's got a golden chain mail little purse
chock full of pennies.
She keeps track to write it off her taxes.
Lottery players pray to her,
"Money, with your heart of gold
pure as McDonald's golden arches,
bless this ticket.
I heard you blow numbers in my ear
like the Virgin Mary heard the Holy Ghost
and I believe."
Money, everyone wants her.
She builds cloud castles on mountains
and funds wars to conquer them.
She builds sand castles

in the sand running out of an hourglass.
And we've all stayed up late at night writing a love poem
about what we'd do with her.
How our hands can make cold cash hot.
Money, no one may judge her. She's like fire.
Burn down a forest or cook your food.
She has no say in how she's used.
Money, she's only the bright dream
of a 7 year old boy
digging up his mother's rosebushes
for buried pirate loot.

TOO LATE

I couldn't sleep.
I stared at white plaster walls
till pictures swam in and out of my eyes.
I saw monsters building an ark
against the rain of fire.
They didn't watch tv,
they'd received a sign from slime.
Vampires wept blood,
the bogeyman wept worms
all the monsters wept for us.
40 days and 40 nights of fire
and no more people.
The ship was made of skeletons
with a gravestone anchor and sails
stretched with shrouds
so monsters would have something
to remember us by.
They'd brought provisions,
hordes of rabid rats
but no children,
tender screaming children.
Just as I fell asleep I thought
"The monsters look so lonely.
What will they do without us?"

DEATH AND STREET TEENAGERS

Street teenagers cuddle in Death's black cape
for safety. Like baby ducks.
His bony fingers play with their spiky mohawks,
from long and thin to long and thin.
Soft throats hung with chains
and a lock their boyfriend closed
but the girls close their eyes
and imagine Death's little fingernail
picking that lock and it opens.
And so do their knees.
They hide his grinning skull between their warm breasts.
So cold and breathless, so exciting.
They argue over bands but they all agree
Death is the cutest, they can't get enough of him.
They put him on t-shirts, tattoos,
they want their skin close to him at all times.
Street teenagers want Death's immortal arms around them
for comfort
when their parents tell them
to stop acting like children.

JURY DUTY

I got a notice to report for jury duty.
I didn't want to go.
The last time I almost got on a jury
the suspect was obviously guilty
of everything except the crime he was charged with,
that crime required brains and planning.
The suspect screamed, waved big clumsy fists
till a sheriff shoved close against him.
The suspect swore at the judge and both lawyers.
His own lawyer kept pulling her tidy dress
away from his flying spittle
and the jury pool wanted to lock him up
'cause he was an obnoxious meanie.
I didn't really want to be stuck explaining
he was a *stupid* obnoxious meanie
and the real criminal had floor plans of the house
and knew the people's vacation schedule.
This guy probably knocked down little old ladies
and stole their purses
and I didn't like him either.
He was one of a pile of cockroaches
crawling in Blind Justice's scales,
too busy fighting to admire her bare brass breasts.
I called the night before and a recorded voice
told me my group number would not be needed
for another year. I'm glad.
I spent a happy day in the sun
and got myself a toasted onion bagel with cream cheese.
But I felt lightning travel down Justice's sword
and burn her cold fingers.
I heard pounding rain drown whatever scuttles in her scales.
No tape recording can tell me what is needed.
Blood trickles from under Justice's blindfold.
It hurts us to look at each other;
it hurts her to look at us.

THE SKIN OF SEEING

Magnolias thrust huge fleshy flowers into summer heat,
escaping from a jealous army of shiny leaves,
as if they'd grown around a girl's breast.
The curve is exact, god practiced skin on flowers
before he got it right.
A tree of breasts half-hidden by moist petals.
They do not beg for hands.
No nipple aches.
God did not make these breasts for love
only beauty.
Beauty so clean it can cut us open
like a butcher's knife.
God's knuckles nudge our guts,
bleeding light.
But enough girls flower on the street
wearing halters in the same heat dazzle
with silver bellybutton rings and boyfriends.
Laughter. Sweet fumbling.
We don't even see what's wasted,
thrown in front of our feet for our eyes to step upon.
Magnolia trees we don't look at
above a world we don't look at.
The soul needs glasses.

TAROT READERS ON THE STREET

On every corner. Rickety folding tables
covered with purple velvet. Or a lace shawl.
Some wear turbans bought at flea markets.
Some wear handmade black capes patched
with lopsided, drunken-looking stars.
Some wear a highwayman's hat with a huge tickling plume
no bird would be caught dead with.
The cards. An occasional crystal.
A chair waiting for you.
"Have facts been bruising you every rushed breakfast?
Are you thrown down the garbage disposal you promised to fix?
Is the new guy at work smiling too much?
Sit. The cards have noble dangers you'll avoid
thru the power hidden in your lowered eyes.
Look up and watch the world catch its breath.
You will meet a mysterious stranger in the mirror,
keep looking until you recognize yourself.
The nightmare won't ride you tonight,
you'll ride her, bareback.
You'll take a long journey all night
over ruined gardens on the moon
and bring home a bouquet of smiles.
Don't use them where they'll do the most good,
waste them magnificently.
Of course you don't believe me,
what have the things you believed got you?
Hang out with the hanged man.
Throw a stick for the fool's dog to chase over the cliff.
Remember when you built the falling tower for your son
from a house of cards; he laughed and hugged you when it fell?
Now he slams doors and stays out late.
I know nothing about you. I care nothing.
But the cards cannot forget you
the way you've forgotten yourself.
Remember," the cards whisper. "Remember."

PEOPLE'S PARK, IN SPITE OF EVERYTHING

There are fights over free box clothes
which can be sold
and are grabbed like piles of pirate loot.
Sometimes the box burns down;
who else wears clothes that start fires?
Who else glows in the dark?
Even sunflowers steal backpacks.
A few white apple blossoms drift
into the mouth of a sleeping drunk,
he wakes, sputtering.
Mostly kids stay out of the park.
Many oldtimers left town.
It's stupid to praise. I hear the earthworms sing.
This is praise.
At our concerts when the music's good enough
and the sound system isn't gargling elephant farts
scars dance on a face before we kick off our shoes
and smiles lick our toes.
Legends aren't here and they won't go away.
Some play at being vampires
but sell our own blood at the end of the month.
Some pose for unwanted posters
but that's just our day job.
This is never a place of peace.
This is a place
of "once upon a time".

POEM

How did joy get caught in ice
like a prehistoric wooly mammoth
with ridiculous feet and shining eyes?
Why are termites eating the kisisng tree?
Did water hate all those people it killed?
If I wait on this corner long enough
someone will ask me for money
to make me go away.
Why don't we look up, do fish-hooks come from the sky
to catch our eyes?
I want to make love in a tub full of deep, ripe cherries,
that color, at least, must be saved from war.
Where is the dictionary of what we do not say?
Why do snakes slither out of telephones
when people talk about being reasonable?
Spiderweb cities glitter; the wind, a broom, a bomb,
gone the people who spent all their lives
not quite escaping.
When we look in mirrors why don't they break?
Sunlight blesses dead tires in a vacant lot
like communion wine in church.
I'm trying to reach my hand thru this paper,
it's a long way.
A laugh, shaken hair and the side of a neck
and nobody was ever hungry.
Where do our fingerprints go when we dream?
The horses from a merry-go-round escaped once
into the tall mountains, golden hooves clanging
and tossing barber poles from the holes in their backs.
They joined a herd of wild horses and drank from streams
where snow melted,
and sometimes they were shot for pet food.
We're all pieces of a jigsaw puzzle
that doesn't fit.
I want a gun that only kills clocks.
Memories don't flush down the toilet,

at least not for very long.
I can't scold the world as if I wasn't in it.
Lonely squats on the sky like a toad on a lilypond,
all our words fill up with water.
Who ate the promises we left behind us
like Hansel and Gretel's breadcrumbs?
Why don't we juggle oranges, burning roses and brass bands
while we talk anymore?
Everything else is just an excuse.
I remember kissing the wind.
Sometimes I can't forgive peartrees
for going right on flowering,
but why should they care about us?
When will we care about us?

Julia Vinograd is a Berkeley street poet. She has published 51 books of poetry, and won the American Book Award of The Before Columbus Foundation. She has three poetry CD collections: *Bubbles and Bones*, *Eye of the Hand*, and *The Book of Jerusalem*. She received a B.A. from the University of California at Berkeley and an M.F.A. from the University of Iowa. She received the 2004 Poetry Lifetime Achievement Award from the City of Berkeley. She was one of the four editors of the anthology *New American Underground Poetry Vol. 1: The Babarians of San Francisco - Poets from Hell*.

Selected Titles Available from Zeitgeist-Press

Where's My Wife **by Jennifer Blowdryer** $5.95
Trek To The Top Of The World **by Andy Clausen** $5.95
Some Angels Wear Black, **by Eli Coppola** $13.95
The Cities of Madame Curie **by Laura Conway** $9.95
My Body Is A War Toy **by Joie Cook** $5.95
Undercover **by Harry Fagel** $14.00
As For Us **by David Gollub** $5.95
how sweet it is **by q. r. hand, jr.** $5.95
The Satin Arcane **by Jack Hirschman** $5.95
The Last Five Miles to Grace, **by David Lerner** $11.95
Pirate Lerner CD **by David Lerner** $10.00
Ghosts Among the Neon **by Bruce Isaacson** $11.95
Going For The Low Blow **by Vampyre Mike Kassel** $5.95
The New American Underground Poetry: The Babarians of San Francisco–Poets From Hell, ed. **Julia Vinograd, David Lerner, and Alan Allen** $23.00
The Queen of Shade **by Sparrow 13 LaughingWand** $5.95
Outlaw of The Lowest Planet **by Jack Micheline** $8.95
The Hummingbird Graveyard **by Maura O'Connor** $5.95
Westering Angels **by Eliot Schain** $15.00
Ask A Mask **by Julia Vinograd** $9.95
Beside Myself **by Julia Vinograd** $9.95
The Cutting Edge **by Julia Vinograd** $9.95
Skull and Crosswords **by Julia Vinograd** $9.95
Step Into My Parlour **by Julia Vinograd** $9.95
Evil Spirits and Their Secretaries **by David West** $5.95
Dogs In Lingerie **by Danielle Willis** $11.95
Tenderloin Rose **by Kathleen Wood** $5.95

Zeitgeist Press
327 Carlisle Crossing St.
Las Vegas, NV 89138 U.S.A.
Postage and handling fees apply. Information & ordering at:
www.zeitgeist-press.com